Walter Wharton's
LAND SURVEY REGISTER
1675-1679

JAMES, DUKE OF YORK
Governor of the Province of New York.

Walter Wharton's
Land Survey Register
1675-1679

WEST SIDE DELAWARE RIVER, FROM NEWCASTLE COUNTY, DELAWARE INTO BUCKS COUNTY, PENNSYLVANIA

Now First Printed

Edited by

ALBERT COOK MYERS

Formerly Chairman of the Historical Committee of the *Valley Forge Park Commission* and Secretary of *The Pennsylvania Historical Commission* of the Commonwealth of Pennsylvania, Ex-President of the *Pennsylvania Federation of Historical Societies*, Ex-President of the *Friends' Historical Society* (England).

Southern Historical Press, Inc.
Greenville, South Carolina

SOUTHERN HISTORICAL PRESS, INC.
PO BOX 1267
Greenville, SC   29601

ISBN #0-89308-273-2

Printed in the United States of America

TO

MY LONG TIME HISTORICAL FRIEND

PIERRE S. DuPONT

(1870–1954)

OF LONGWOOD GARDENS, WHO READ THE
MANUSCRIPT OF THIS BOOK AND WAS
INSTRUMENTAL IN HAVING IT PRINTED.

ALBERT COOK MYERS

ILLUSTRATIONS

SIR EDMUND ANDROS
Deputy Governor of the Province of New York.

INTRODUCTION[1]

A pulping machine of a York County paper plant[2] was about to devour this precious old manuscript Land Survey Register of Surveyor Walter Wharton, of over two and three quarters of a century ago. Just in the nick of time the Register was rescued[3] by a workman attracted by the antique handwriting.

The Register, nearly all of it in the copperplate hand of Wharton himself, consists of fifty recorded descriptive surveys of the metes and bounds of tracts of land

[1] Abbreviations: R.C.N.C.—Printed *Records of the Court of New Castle on Delaware.* 1676–1681 (1904).

[2] The Glatfelter Paper Company, of Spring Grove, York County, Pennsylvania, to which it had been sold by a Harrisburg junk dealer.

[3] The rescue of the Register is a reminder of the recovery of another early historical document of prime interest, as recounted in my book *William Penn, His Own Account of the Lenni Lenape or Delaware Indians, 1683* (Moylan, Pa., 1937), pages 93–94.

In 1924, when I was concerned with the work of erecting a stone and bronze marker to Quonemysing Indian Town of Chief Secetareous on Brandywine Creek, near the Circular

for the period 1675–1679. In parts much tattered, torn and water-stained the document comprises 36 written pages, including the original index, of unbound sheets of old paper, in size 8 x 12 inches.

The area of the surveyings extends for about 56 miles, from St. Georges Creek, now New Castle County, Delaware, on the south, as far north as Neshaminy Creek, now Bucks County, Pennsylvania.

This region was then known as West Side Delaware River, now comprising the

---

Line of Delaware (see *Marking the Historic Sites of Early Pennsylvania*, 4th Report of the Pennsylvania Historical Commission, 1926, pages 39–41), I had sought in vain for the original deed of the Chief to William Penn for the land "between Christina and Upland [Chester] Creek," in 1683, when, to my joy, the late LeRoy Harvey (1873–1928), Mayor of Wilmington, hastened to me in Pennsylvania, informing me of his finding the original deed. Forthwith, he motored me to New Castle, Delaware, where, upon the dining room table of the late Mrs. Francis de H. Janvier (1873–1940, *nee* Annie Read Rodney, sister of Judge Richard S. Rodney), atop a heap of torn papers in four torn pieces lay the lost deed. Mrs. Janvier, all honor to her, had hunted it out of peach baskets of discarded papers from the next-door home

Sealed & delivered ye 14 June An° 1683

Secretarius & ... Nickholas & Nockcotamon & Toonis
& Eeghanan & Swanpuis do Hereby promiss & Engage to give
& grant all our Land lying between Christina & Upland Creek
on ... Land lying between Christina & Upland Creek
unto William Penn Propriatary & Govern° of Pennsilvania
... of Pennsilvania, as for ... manner as ... Heirs ... & other
... ... in ... price ... :
... Goods already receive a very good ... ... Sea two
pair of Stockins, one Matchcoat & ... bitty ... mon[e]y
in witness ... ... my Hand & Seal.

Secretarius   Ph° Mark

witnessed in ... of
Swen ...
Tho. Holme
John Moone
Lasse Cock

Recto of Indian Deed in the hand of William Penn: "Secetareus and Kalcup or Kailops deed about Christeen."

QUEONEMYSING
INDIAN TOWN
WAS LOCATED ON
THE OTHER SIDE OF
BRANDYWINE CREEK FROM HERE
IN THE GREAT BEND
RATTLESNAKE TRAIL
LED THENCE OVER POINT LOOKOUT
TO THE ROCKS ON CHRISTINA CREEK
IN PRESENT WILMINGTON
THE CHIEF
SECETAREUS
AND HIS PEOPLE
OF THE UNAMI GROUP
★ THEIR TOTEM ★ THE TORTOISE ★
OF THE LENNI – LENAPE OR DELAWARES
SOLD TO
WILLIAM PENN
THE LAND BETWEEN
CHESTER CREEK AND CHRISTINA CREEK
DECEMBER 19, 1683

MARKED BY
THE PENNSYLVANIA HISTORICAL COMMISSION
AND THE DELAWARE COUNTY HISTORICAL SOCIETY
1924

Queonemysing Indian Town Marker Tablet

Queonemysing Indian Town Marker, on Brandywine Creek, about
3 miles South of Chadds Ford, Pennsylvania.

Site of Queonemysing Indian Town of Chief Seectareus, in the Great Bend of Brandywine Creek, in present Delaware County, Pennsylvania, just over the Circular Line of Delaware State.

States of Delaware and Pennsylvania. It was a part of the government of the Province of New York. James, Duke of York (1633–1701), was the Governor of the whole territory. Sir Edmund Andros (1637–1714) was the Deputy Governor with his residence in New York.

The Register was a state document, a part of the official archives for the region. A Domesday Book, as it were, of land records and a bead-roll of early settlers for the era, it is of real basic historical value and interest and of legal importance

---

of the late Alexander B. Cooper (1844–1924), historian of New Castle. The old paper is item No. 1552 in a list of over two thousand documents transferred, in 1801, by legislative act from the State of Pennsylvania to Delaware. William Penn's handwriting is on the back of the deed.

I had the deed skillfully restored in Philadelphia for Mrs. Janvier and, by her courtesy, I was permitted to reproduce it for the first time in my above William Penn book. The document is now owned by Mrs. Janvier's daughter, Mrs. Walter Pyle, Jr., of Old Mill Lane, Stanton, Delaware.

In 1685, Penn sent over from England as a gift a cap to the Chief. Caleb Pusey (1650–1726), of Chester, in his unprinted holograph History of Pennsylvania gives an interesting account of a visit to the Chief at Quonemysing.

as an initial land title record for that region.[4]

As far as I have noted, eight of the surveys, as indicated in the text, have been printed previously, as follows (the page numbers in marks of parenthesis refer to the Register):

I. In Dr. George Smith's (1804–1884), *History of Delaware County* (Philadelphia, 1862, a most reliable work), five, on pages (16), (19), (20), (31) and (32), on pages 521–523, as "From an old Book of Surveys, Surveyor General's Office, Harrisburg," but with variants and errors. Dr. Smith was assisted by his son, Benjamin H. Smith, (1841–1918, engineer, author of an admirable *Atlas of the Early Settlements of Delaware County*, Philadelphia, 1880. I knew him).

II. In *The Duke of York Book*, 1646–1679 (Wilmington, Delaware, 1903) three,

---

[4] Wharton also surveyed land over Delaware River on Cohansey Creek, in New Jersey.—R.C.N.C., 430–432.

on pages (21), at pages 33–34, page (5) at page 34, page (21) at pages 34–35.

In the *Records of the Court of New Castle on Delaware*, 1676–1681, (Lancaster, Pa., 1904), under date of December 3, 1678, pages 267–268, Walter Wharton made return to the Court of three surveys that are not entered in his Register.

In the *Record of the Court of Upland* (Philadelphia, 1860), edited by Edward Armstrong (1818–1874), "Wharton's Surveys, 20th Sept., 1675, Surveyor Genl's Office, Harrisburg" is cited, page 115; another reference on page 198.

The following is a list of seven of Walter Wharton's surveys not recorded in his Register but copied into the *Record* and printed: September, 1677, warrant from the Court to Michael Izard, pages 121–122; September 1677, warrant from the Court to Anthony Nielson, alias Long, pages 122-123; October 8, 1678, survey to James Sandelandes and Lawrence Cock, page 123; October 12, 1678, survey to Pieter Rambo, Jr., pages 123-124; November 1677, order of the Court, to Jacobson Hendrickson, pages 124–125; October 10, 1678, survey to Henry Hastings, page 125; September 27, 1678, survey to John Test, page 126.

Walter Wharton was an Englishman.[5] As surveyor, justice of the courts, and as citizen he figures in the records of the West Side Delaware River as one of the notables of his period and active in its affairs.[6] How much he was to the fore is shown by the many references in the index to the printed *Records of the Court of New Castle, 1676–1681.*

---

[5] According to his oath at the confirmation of his office as surveyor at the Dutch Conquest in 1673, hereafter cited.

[6] Dr. George Smith sketches him in his *History of Delaware County, Pa.* (Philadelphia, 1862), 510.

A single man, he had come to live in the region, it would seem, as early as 1671, for on April 15, of that year, Captain John Carr, resident in charge of the government on the Delaware, came before the Council of New York, at Fort James, and reported "the Desire of many Families to come & settle below New Castle at Apoquiminy & Bomboys Hook, to be Consider'd of. The most eminent amongst them are Mr Jones Mr Wharton, Mr Whate, A Letter is Order'd to be written to Treat wth them ab^t their Settlem.^{tm}"[7]

On June 16, 1671 Francis Lovelace (1630–1707), Deputy Governor of New York, at Fort James, signed a land patent deed to Walter Wharton for 400 acres of land, "on ye North East side of a Creek now called St Jones his Creek being about a Mile above Murder Creek, & extendeth it self North West from" Delaware Bay; "Bounded on ye South West wth ye said

---

[7] *Pa. Arch.*, 2 S.V. 623.

Creek, and on the South East wth ye Land of Mr Robert Jones, & on two opposite sides wth ye Main Woods. "[8]

And on June 17, 1671, Governor Lovelace commissioned Walter Wharton Surveyor General "in Delaware River, that is to say of the Western Side of said River." It "hath been Customary," reads the commission, "& is thought very convenient that some known person skilfull in the Mathematicks and well understanding in the Art of Surveying shou'd be appointed and Sworn Surveyor to Measure or Lay out Lands or Lots of Ground in Delaware River, wch shall at any time be Ordered by me". Governor Lovelace has "a good opinion of the Capacity, Integrity and Ability of Mr. Walter Wharton for that Employment."[9]

---

[8] D. S. of Francis Lovelace, a patent deed in Logan Papers, vol. 24:9, in HSP.

[9] Albany Records, Court of Assizes, Vol. II:378; *Pa. Arch.* 2 S.V. 628–629; Samuel Hazard's *Register*, 387.

The Council at Fort James, January 27, 1672, appointed "Capt" Walter Wharton one of the four appraisers in the celebrated suit of Armegot, widow of Johan Papegoja (daughter of Johan Printz, the Swedish first Governor, 1643–1653, in present Pennsylvania) against Carr as to the title of the Island of Tinicum.[10] He "was made a justice" "on Delaware River," April 6, 1672.[11]

With the Dutch Conquest of New York and the Delaware, in 1673, Wharton was continued in office by Captain Anthony Colve, the new Governor General of New Netherland. The commission, dated September 25, 1673, at Fort Willem Hendrick, in New Netherland, recites that Walter Wharton, "Land Surveyor in the South River (Delaware River) of New Netherland," is of "good report". On

---

[10] *Pa. Arch.* V. (1890) 655–6.

[11] Sketch of Wharton in *Publications of the Genealogical Society of Pennsylvania*, Vol. I, No. 1, January, 1895. Source for this not found by me.

September 26, 1673, "I Walter Wharton Surveyor off the South River here to fore Called dellewarr" took the oath of office.[12]

The English returning to power, Governor Andross, August 14, 1677, appointed Wharton Surveyor for the Delaware[13], and September 23 of that year commissioned him one of the justices of the Court of New Castle; the following October 6, he took the oath of office and sat in the Court at New Castle.[14]

At the Court, March 7, 1678, the clergy of the Town presented Wharton "for marrying himselfe," "Contrary to ye knowne Laws."[15] From this and later entries of the Record for the year evidently he was quite unwell and unable to fulfill his obligations. Business and other

---

[12] *Pa. Arch.* 2 S.V. 664–665.

[13] *Pa. Arch.* V. 728.

[14] R.C.N.C. 144–145.

[15] R.C.N.C. 179, 210–211.

troubles beset him. He died in New Castle January 3, 1679.[16] Dominie Petrus Teschemacker, of New Castle, preached his funeral sermon at a charge of 50 gilders.[17] Dr. Thomas Spry, "Chirurgeon", was paid 262 gilders for "Phisicq" for Wharton[18] and Ralph Hutchinson, of the Town, received 814 gilders for Wharton's "meat, drink and lodging" and 1220 gilders for his sickness and funeral charges.[19]

January 8, 1679, upon the petition of Mary Wharton, the widow, the Court appointed Captain Edmund Cantwell, of New Castle, as administrator on Wharton's estate.[20]

---

[16] Sketch of him in *Publications of the Genealogical Society of Pennsylvania*, Vol. I, Jan., 1895, pages 36–37.

[17] R.C.N.C., 321, 478.

[18] R.C.N.C. 316, 382. See John F. Lewis, *Thomas Spry, Lawyer and Physician* (Philadelphia, 1932).

[19] R.C.N.C. 337–338.

[20] R.C.N.C. 277, 280–281.

Walter Wharton and his wife seemed to have lived chiefly in New Castle Town, where his last days were spent. He had a house and lot in the Town south of the Old Block House, between Minquas or Susquehanna Street on the west and Warmoes or Land Street on the east, and between the lot of Johannes de Haes to the south and William Orian to the North.[21]

He also owned a plantation of 600 acres located on Blackbird Creek, a branch of Duck Creek. This is the inventory of this property, appraised in 1679 by Gerrett Otto and Caspares Herrman:

	gilders
3 Cowes	570
3 beasts of 2 year old	300
2 yearly Calves at 40 gilders	80
1 ditto att	50
6 young shotes 2 young sowes 1 old sowe	160

[21] See Leon de Valinger, Jr., Map of New Castle in 1682, issued in 1932.

2 yron Potts and 1 frying pan	90
1 payle 5 bowles 1 pewter bason	35
1 bed Rugg & blancket	80
In pouder and shott	14
1 Crass Kutsawe	30
1 pr of mill stones	40
1 remnant of stuf a Cake of soape & some thread	70
1 chest 1 barrill i tub	
1 tinn Cullander 1 old sadle & Cloaths	24
7 prs of hinges & some other small Laches	20
2 sighs	30
1 hammer 1 Reipe hooke 2 plaine yrons	8
2 Cocks and 3 hins	6
1 broad ax	5
The Plantation being 600 acres Lying in blakebird Creeke att	2600

Gilders 4232[22]

---

[22] R.C.N.C. 298–299.

Furthermore, his estate was charged 80 gilders rent of a house of Marmaduke Randall in Upland (later Chester).[23]

Thirty years ago I was a member of The Pennsylvania Historical Commission of The Commonwealth of Pennsylvania, appointed (January 18, 1924) by Governor Gifford Pinchot (1865–1946), during his first term. I was elected Secretary of the Commission, and, supported by the Chairman, Colonel Henry W. Shoemaker, was given full direction of the Commission's activities. At that time I obtained a photostatic copy[24] of the original Register. My photostat includes not alone all of the rescued book but also the missing lower half of a leaf, pages (1) and (2) of the Register, with the signatures of Walter Wharton. (See reproductions fol-

---

[23] *Record of the Court of Upland, Penna.,* 1676–1681. (Philadelphia, 1860), 130.

[24] Through the courtesy of Dr. Hiram H. Shenk (1872–1954), then Custodian of the Public Records, State Library, Harrisburg, Pennsylvania.

lowing pages 26 and 30.) This missing fragment, in 1926, I found stuck fast, at that time, in the metal file, marked "Philadelphia Lots", in the State Land Office where it had been kept before the book was discarded.

With authority to print, at that time I had the whole of the photostatic copy typed, checked it personally and prepared for printing the text now here presented. Circumstances then prevented publication, and during this interval my manuscript has been in my hands awaiting favorable opportunity for its issue.

ALBERT COOK MYERS[25]

Moylan, Delaware County, Pennsylvania

December 12, 1954

---

[25] See sketch in *Who's Who in America*, for 1950–1951, Vol. 26, page 1989.

NOTE

The Register in the main is new information. It will be found a useful supplement to the following works: *Records of the Court of New Castle on Delaware, 1676–1681* (Lancaster, Pa., 1904, 200 copies); *Records of the Court of New Castle on Delaware, 1681–1699*, Vol. II, edited by Albert Cook Myers (Meadville, Pa., 1935, 500 copies); *The Duke of York Record, 1646–1679* (Wilmington, Delaware, 1903); *Record of the Court of Upland, 1676–1681*, edited by Edward Armstrong (Philadelphia, 1860); *Record of the Courts of Chester County, Pennsylvania, 1681–1697* (Philadelphia, 1910); *Records of the Courts of Quarter Sessions and Common Pleas of Bucks County, Pennsylvania, 1684–1700* (Meadville, Pa., 1943, 500 copies); Samuel Hazard, *Annals of Pennsylvania, 1609-1682* (Philadelphia, 1850); Albert Cook Myers, "Pennsylvania Historical Exhibit," at the Jamestown Exposition, 1907, pages 98-281, in *Pennsylvania at the Jamestown Exposition, Hampton Roads, Va: 1907* (Philadelphia. Published by the Pennsylvania Commission, 1908, 8 vo., 360 pages); Albert Cook Myers, *Narratives of Early Pennsylvania, West New Jersey and Delaware, 1630-1707* (Scribner's, New York, 1912).

Transcript of
Walter Wharton's
Land Survey Register
1675–1679

(1)

Surveyed the 27th of May 1675 for M^{rs}: Wale[1] three hund (Torn ⅝ inch) of Land called Chelsey, Scituate on the W[est] (Torn ½ inch) Side of Delaware River and on the Sou[th] (Torn ¾ inch) Side of St Georges Creek, being the first [neck of][2] (Torn ¾ inch) firme Land

---

[1] Mrs. Anna Wale.

[2] These two words are supplied from New Castle Court minutes.

[3] Number 33 as here given to the Register, in 1765, by John Hughes (—1772) then recorder of the land records in the Land Office of the Province of Pennsylvania. He was a prominent and prosperous Philadelphia Official—*Statutes at Large of Pennsylvania* V. 1744-1759, pages 448-455; Pa. Arch. 2 S. XIX (1890) 673; Scharf and Westcott, *Philadelphia*, I. 271.

[3]Number Thirty three ⅌ Jo^n Hughes

within the said Creek and is bo[unded].
(Torn ¾ inch) as followeth: Begining at
a Corn^r m^{r}k^d. Oa[k] Standing on a point
by ye North Side of a Sw[amp]. (Torn ¼
inch) wch divideth this from a parcell of
Land form[erly] (Torn ¼ inch) granted
to Mr Peter Alricks: and from y^e (Torn
¼ inch) runing up by the Said Swamp
W by N: (Torn ¼ inch) eight perches
N: Westerly 25 degrees 28 (Torn ¼ inch)
N: W: 88 perches; S W: 32 perches
W by (Torn ¼ inch) perches S by W 34
perches: E S [W]: 60 pe[rches] S W: 40
perches W by S 24 perches to a (Faded
½ inch) M^{r}ked Gum standing By y^e
head of a branch of (Faded ⅜ inch)
Swamp, and from ye said Gum runing
W: S: W: [by] Line of m^{r}ked trees: 133
perches to a Corn^r M^r[ked] White Oak:
Standing nigh unto th (Torn 1¼ inches)
Swamp or branch, And from (Torn 1¾
inches) N N W: 150 perches to a Co (Torn

Reproduction of a phostat, made in 1926, of the verso of the leaf, the lower part of page (1) of the original manuscript Register. This piece had tore off and stuck fast in the metal file marked "Philadelphia Lots" when the Register was discarded from the Land Office. This missing part of the Register is now here included in its printing. Walter Wharton's signature with four final letters torn off.

2 inches) nigh unto the head of a (Torn
2¾ inches) Swamp and from (Torn 3½
inches) line (Torn 4½ inches)
(The rest of the page, 4⅝ inches long,
torn off.)

(The verso of the torn off leaf, page (1).
See reproduction here)

Survey[ed] (Torn off 4 inches) Crawford 210 (Torn off 4 inches) y² Westward
s[id]e of Delaware [River] (Torn 1 inch)
ward side of [Ge]orges Creek: Being
[from ?] NE and N [xxx] with yᵉ maine
Creck on the South East with a Swamp
Called the Docto[rs] and on the south
West: with a Line mʳ[kd] trees: Running
from a Cornʳ mʳkᵈ Black [oak] Standing
on a point oppoos[ite] (Torn off 2 inches)
Plantation S S E : to a Cornʳ (Faded 2
inches) By a Branch of yᵉ afore Said
Swamp (Torn 1 inch) this said quantity

of Land together (Torn 1 inch) Marshes thereto Adioyneing:

℔ me   Walt^r. Wha (Torn off ¾ inch)

By order & Appointmt of Capt (Torn off ¾ inch) Cantwell Survey^r.

(2)

Surveyed the 28th: day of May 1675 For Mr Thomas Spry[4] One hundred and Sixty Acres of Land called Doctors Commons Scituate on ye Westward side of Delaware River and on the Southward side of St Georges Creek: being bounded as followeth vizt: Begining at a Corn^r M^rk white oak: Standing Close by ye Creek side at ye first firme Land w^thin ye s^d Creek: dividing this from ye Land of Mrs Ann Wa[le.] (Torn ⅜ inch) and from y^e

-----

[4] See John F. Lewis, *Thomas Spry Lawyer* and *Physician* (Philadelphia, 1932).

said oak runing West South West By Mrs: Wales line of mrked trees three hundred and eighty Perches to a Cornr mrked black oak Standing by the side of a Swamp called ye Doctors Swamp * * * unto ye head thereof and from ye said black oak downe the Severall Courses of ye maine run of ye Said Swamp unto ye affore Said Creek and then downe ye Severall Courses of ye Creek to the first mentioned white oak Conteyneing the Said Quantity of Land togeather with the Marshes thereto Adioyneing:

> ℔ me   Waltr: Wharton
> By order & appointment of
> Capt. Edmond Cantwell
> Surveyr.

(Torn 3¼ inches) of May 1675 for Ja (Torn ½ inch) (Torn 4½ inches) Scituate (Rest of page, 4⅝ inches long, torn off).

(The recto of the torn leaf, page (2). See reproduction here)

[S]wamp called (Faded ¾ inch) [s]aid black Oak E (Faded ¼ inch) [M]ked trees 380 perches: to a (Faded ¼ inch) white oak Standing on yᵉ banck of the sai[d] and divideth this from a parcell of land now for Thomas Spry and from yᵉ Said White Oak (Faded ¼ inch) the Severall Courses of yᵉ Creek to the River and (Faded ¼ inch) er Westerly along the aforementioned [S]wamp thorow yᵉ Marsh to yᵉ first ment[ioned] [Cornʳ?] white Oak Conteyning yᵉ Said quan[tity] of Land and also yᵉ Marshes thereto Adoynei[ng]

℔ Waltʳ. Wharton
By order & Appointment of
Capᵗ Edmond Cantwell
Surveyoʳ.

(3)

Surveyed ye 29th: day of May 1675 for (Torn ¼ inch) George More 280 acres of Land (Faded ½ inch) Woodl[and] (Faded ¼ inch) Scituate on ye Westward side of Dela[ware.] (Faded 1 inch) and on ye South Side of St Georges Creek (Faded 1 inch) to Mr Jacob Youngs Plantation Being (Faded 1 inch) on ye E N E with a line of M^rk^ed tre[es Run] (Faded ½ inch) ing S S E from a Corn^r m^rked Black oak (Faded ½ inch) ye bounded tree of ye Land of James Craw[ford.] (Faded ½ inch) dividing this from ye said Crawfords Land on y^e (Faded ½ inch) N W: with ye maine Creek; On ye W S (Faded ¾ inch) with a line of m^rked trees Runing from a (Faded ½ inch) m^rked white oak on a point by ye Creeks side S S E. 314 pearches: to a Corn^r m^rked Maple Standing in a branch of ye Doct^rs Swamp and on ye S S E with

ye said swamp Conteyneing the quantity
of Land togeather wth ye Marshes there
(Faded ¼ inch) Adioyneing:

〜 me Walt^r. Wharton
By order & Appointment (of)
Capt. Ed (Faded ¼ inch) Cantwell
Survey^r.

Surveyed: ye 29th day of May 1675 for
[John Ogle] (Faded 1 inch) three hundred
acres of Land called Hamptons Sw[amp]
(Faded ¼ inch) on ye Westward Side of
Delaware River and on Southward (Faded
¼ inch) side of St Georges Creek being
bounde[d] on ye N N W: with a branch of
ye Said Creek wch extendeth it selfe W S W.
out of ye maine Creek: on ye E N E:
w[ith] a line of m^{r}ked trees runing S S E:
divid[ing] (Torn 1 inch) ye Land of George
More on the W S W: (Faded ½ inch)
(Torn ½ inch) Line of m^{r}ked trees Runing S. E: from a Corn^r (Faded ¼ inch) a

white oak at ye mouth of a small Creeple dividing this from a parcell of Land now Surveyed for [Ber]nard Egberts and on ye South South east with (Faded ¾ inch) woods.

℔ Walt^r. Wharton

(4)

Surveyed ye 29th: day of May 1675 for Bernard Egberts three hundred Acres of Land Called Black Smiths hall Scituate on ye Westward Side of Delaware River and on ye Southward Side of S^t. Georges Creek, towards the head of a branch wch. extendeth it selfe W S W. out of ye maine Creek Being bounded on the N N W: with the Said branch On ye E N E with a Line of m^rked trees dividing this from the Land of John Ogle on the W S W with a line drawne S S E: from a Corn^r m^rked whit[e] Oak on a low point at ye mouth of a Small Swamp and on y^e

S S E with the maine Woods Including the said quantity of Land:

Surveyed ye 9th. day of July 1675: for Olie ffranson[5], Marcus Lawrenson & Miele Mielson Seaven hundred Acres of Land Scituate on ye westward side of Delaware River: About two miles aboue Vedrietie hook: in a place called ye Bowght: Begining at a Corn^r m^{r}ked white oak Standing at the North East Side of the mouth of a small Creek Called Dogg Creek, and from the Said white Oak: runing North West by a line of m^{r}ked trees: dividing this from ye land of Charles Peterson 320 perches: to a Corn^r m^{r}ked White oak, standing nigh onto ye head of a branch of a Creek Called storry Creek and from thence runing N E by a line of m^{r}ked trees 390 perches to another Corn^r m^{r}ked white

---

[5] Olie Franson.

oak: standing by ye head of a branch of ye Bowght Creek, called Popler branch: and from ye said oak runing downe ye seuerall Courses: of ye s^d branch and Creek to ye maine river: And finally downe By ye R[iver Si]de to ye first mentioned white oak at ye mouth of dog Creek: Conteyne[ing] ye said quantitie of Land: Besides Swamps, and Sunken gro[und] y^t three hundred acres part hereof, being formerly granted unto ye s. Ol[ie ff]ranson, Peter Mounson & Niels Nielson: by patent beareing dat[e] (Torn ¼ inch) (Faded ¼ inch) day of Aprill: 1673: since which time Marcus Lawrenson is (Torn ¾ inch) (Torn ¼ inch) ye right of Peter Mounson) & ye other four hundred acres being (Torn ½ inch) (Torn ⅞ inch) alwaies that ye inhabitants of Vertrieties hook shall haue (Torn ⅞ inch) (Torn ½ inch) and a priviledge of ye Stony Creek & ye Mill which they have

(Torn ⅞ inch) (Torn 1 inch) mann^r as they haue formerly done.

(5)

[6]Surveyed ye 23: day of July 1675: for Thomas Jacobson, Olie Paulson, and Arent Johnson, Two hundred fo[rty] (Faded ½ inch) Eight Acres of Land Called Red Clays point: Scituate on Westward Side of Delaware River And on y^eNorth a[nd] North West side of bread and Cheese Island and is more th[an] (Torn ¼ inch) halfe compassed with a branch of Christinia Creek: Called Red Clayes Creek: begining: at a Corn^r Marked white oak: standing at ye mouth of a small branch of Red Clays Creek called Hearing branch, wch divideth this from the Land of Jacob Johnson: And from the said oak runing North: Eas[t]

[6-6] Printed with variants and omissions in *Duke of York Record*, p. 34.

Seaven degrees up ye said branch or Rivolet: one hundred [and] (Faded ¼ inch) Sixty Perches: then from the Said Rivolet North by a line of m^rked trees: one hundred and sixty perches to a Corn^r M^rked w[hite] (Faded ⅛ inch) oak; standing on a Levell from thence West: by a line of M^rk[ed] trees: One hundred perches to a Cor^r m^rked white oak standing under a high banck by a small Swamp nigh unto the side of re[d] clays Creek and from thence runing downe the several Cours[es] of the said Creek: to the first mentioned whit oak at the mouth of Hearing branch: (viz: one hundred acres part hereof being [for]merly granted unto ye said Thomas Jacobson, Olie Paul[lson] and Tho: Snelling by patent bearing date ye 1st: day of Oct. 1669: Since which time Arent Johnson is Invested [in the] (Torn ½ inch) Right of Thomas Snelling; and

one hundred for[ty] eight Acres the other
part hereof Being new Land:⁶

> ["by me Walter Wharton by
> order of Capt. Ed Cantwell
> Surveyor General."]⁷

(6)

[S]urveyed (the 27ᵗʰ day of August
1675) for Mʳ Lawrentius Carolus: three
hundred and fifty acres of Land called
Teckquorassy Scituate on the Westward
side of Delaware River being the Land
where Ollie Stille hath formerly dwelt:
Bounded as followeth: Viz.ᵗ begining at
a Cornʳ mʳked Popler Standing nigh unto
the old landing in Ollie Stilles Creek: and
from the Said Popler runing along by the
Swamp Side: Which lieth along by yᵉ
River North Easterly: 62 degrees: 144
perches: North East 18 perches North

---

⁷ Additional in *Duke of York Record*, p. 34.

by East 16 perches and North Easterly
62 degrees 98 Perches: to a Corn^r marked
Maple standing by ye Swamp Side: and
divideth this from the Land of Nieles
Matson And from the said Maple North
West by a line of M^{r}ked trees dividing
this from the land of the Said Nieles 338
Perches to a Cor^r m^{r}ked red oak: Standing on a ridge Betweene the afore Said
Creek: and a Creek called Crum Kill:
and from the Said oak: South West 46:
Perches by a line of m^{r}ked trees to a
Corn^r m^{r}ked red oak: Standing by a Small
peice of Marsh at the Side of Ollie Stilles
Creek and from thence downe the severall
Courses of the said Creek: to the first
mentioned Popler Conteyneing the Said
quantitie of Land togeather with the
Medow ground thereto adioyneing; part
of this Said land haueing been granted to
the said Lawrentius Carolus by a former
Patent:

(7)

Surveyed the 24th: of Novemb^r. 1675)
for Mr Peter Co[ck] six hundred and fifty
Acres of land Called Quessina[wo]mink
situate on the Westward side of Delaware
River being bounded as followeth: Viz^t:
begining at Corn^r m^rked Red oak Standing by a piece of Meadow gro[und] being
a bounded tree of the Land of Shakhamexunk (Shackamaxon) and from the
said oak runing N. N. W: by Shakham-
exunk Line of m^rked trees: three hundred
and fifty perches to a corn^r m^rked white
oak: being ye upper corn^r bounded tree
of the said land of Shakhamexunk and
from thence E N E: by a line of marked
trees one hundred and fifty perches to a
corner marked Black oak standing nigh
unto Quessinawomink Creek side opposite
to the mouth of Tawocawomink Creek
and from thence downe the severall
courses of the maine Creek: to the maine

river side and from the mouth of Quessinawomink Creek downe by the river
and by the Swamp or Creeple lying by
the River side to the firs[t] mentioned
Corn^r oak Conteyneing the said quan-
ti[ty] of Land togeather with the Meadow
ground ther[eto] (Torn ½ inch) Adioyneing:

(8)

Surveyed the second day of November
1675: for Lawrence Cock: Erick Cock:
Michael Nielson: Otto Ernest Cock:
Goner Rambo and Peter Nielson a tract
of Land called Shakhamexunk conteyneing sixteene hundred acres: scituate on
the Westward Side of Delaware river
being bounded as followeth: vizt Begining
on a small poin[t] at the mouth of a
Creek called Cohocksink Creek: And
from thenc[e] runing betweene the East
and North East along the river side
according to the severall courses thereof

to a corn^r m^rked red oak Standing by a
piece of Meadow ground and divideth
this from a tract of land called Quessinawomink: belonginge to Peter Cock the
distance from the mouth of the said Creek
to the said oak in a direct line being nine
hundred and twenty perches and from
ye said oak N N W By a line of marked
trees dividing this from the said land of
Peter Cock: Three hundred and fifty
perches to a corn^r m^rked white oak Standing by a small creeple nigh unto ye high
way and from that oak W N W: By a line
of m^rked trees 620: perches to a Corn^r
m^rked Maple standing at the side of the
run of the Westtermost branch of Shakhamexunk Creek: and from thence up
the Severall courses of the said run to a
corn^r m^rked white oak Standing in y^e
Swamp at the North East Side of the run;
and from that oak W S W: By a line of
marked trees 220 Perches to a Corn^r

marked oak Standing at the North East
Side of the Run or maine Branch of
Cohocksinks Creek: and from thence
downe the Severall Courses of the said
Creek to the place of begining conteyneing the said quantity of Land togeather
with the Meadow ground therto Adioyneing Besides the water and Sunken
land therein conteyned 600 acres part
hereof being formerl[y] granted unto
Peter Cock by patent: Bearing date the
5th [day] (Torn ½ inch) of June 1664:
and one thousand Acres the Residue here
[of] (Torn ½ inch) Being New Land:

(9)

Surveyed the 22d day of October 1675:
for Peter Pete[r]son and Gasper ffish a
tract of land conteyneing five hundred
acres, Called Pimmeepahka (Pennypack),
Scituate on the Westward side of Delaware River and on the lower Side of

Pimmeepahka's Creek Being bounded as followeth: vizt Begining at a corner marked black oak Standing by the river side nigh unto the lower end of a peice of Meadow ground and from the Said oak runing North North West by a line of marked trees: three hundred and twenty perches to another Corn^r m^rked black oak: Standing about twenty perches from [y^e] (Torn ⅛ inch) northward side of a small swamp; and from that oak: East north East By a line of marked trees three hundred and Sixty perches to a corn^r marked white oak Standing on ye Banck of Pimmeepahka's Creek about thirty perche[s] aboue the high way: and from the said white oak downe the severall courses of the said Creek to the maine River side and from the mouth of the Said Creek downe along the river Side to the first mentioned black oak: conteyneing the said quantity of land togeather with ye Meadow ground thereto belonging: the Said la[nd] (Torn ¼ inch) being part of a tract of Land formerly granted t[o] Andrew Carr (for one hundred acres more or less By patent bearing date the first day of January 1667:

(10)

Surveyed the 20th day of October 1675 for Erick: Mullock: Olie Nielson and Christian Thomason: a tract of land conteyneing nine hundred and fifty acres: Knowne by the name of Tawocawomink, Scituate on the Westward Side of Delaware river betweene two Creeks the one called Quessinawomink Creek: the other Sissowokissink, being bounded as followeth Viz^t: begining at the river side at the West side of the mouth of Sissowokissink Creek and from thence runing up the said Creek: North Westerly 301 degrees 22 perches: North by East: 28

perches: North North West: 120 perches.
and North 198 perches bounded wth the
Said Creek: to a corner marked white
oak Standing at ye side of the run of the
said Creek by the mouth of a Small
Branch And from the Said oak by a line
of Marked trees: W: 336: perches to a
corn^r m^rked white oak Standing on the
side of a knowle on the Eastward Side of
a branch or Creek called Tawocawomink
Creek: being a branch of Quessinawomink
and from thence downe the severall
courses of the Said branch and maine
Creek to the River Side: and from the
mouth of Quessinawomink Creek, along
by the river Side to the place of begining
Conteyneing the Said quantity of Land—
togeather with the Meadow ground thereto belonging the Said land being part of
a tract of land formerly granted to
Andrew Carr for one hundred acres more
or less by patent bearing date the first
day of Jan^{ry}: 1667.

(11)

Surveyed: the 12th: day of October 1675: for Peter Dalboe: three hundred Acres of land Scituate the westward side of Delaware river and on the Eastward side of the Schuyle Kill: being bounded as followeth Vizt Begining on a point by ye Upper side of a rock at ye mouth of a diep branch nigh and by the dwelling house of the said Dalboe: which said branch divideth this from the land of Pete[r] Ramboe and from the said point Runing by the side of the Said Kill or Creek North Easterly: 30 degrees 156 perches North Easterly 85 degrees: 32 perches: East by South 14: perches: South East 36 perches E S E: 38 perches: North Easterly 81: degrees: 60 perches and North East 36 perches; to a cornr mrked white oak Standing at the Side of the aforesaid Kill or Creek: and from the said oak South East: By a line of mrked trees: two hundred forty and four perches to a corn^r m^rked white oak: Standing on a Barren Levell: and from that oak South west by a line of m^rked trees one hundred and eighty perches to another corn^r m^rked white oak: Standing in the East line of Passayunk land: Being the Uppermost corn^r [of] (Torn ¼ inch) the land of Peter Ramboe and from thence North West of a line of m^rked trees: one hundred and sixty perches to a sma[ll] Swamp: which decendeth into the first mentioned diep branch and from thence NorthWest^r.ly downe the sev[er]all courses of the said Swamp to place of begining the which said line and Swamp divideth this from the Land of the said Ramboe:

(12)

Surveyed: the 23^d day of November 1675: for William Grant four hundred Acres of Land: called Thusk: Scituate on

ye West side of Delaware River: and on
the South side of the maine Branch of
St Georges Creek: aboue the land of John
Scott Being bounded as followeth: Viz^t:
Begining at a corner m^rked white oak:
Standing on a point on the West side of
ye mouth of a branch or Swamp: which
proceedeth out of the said Creek: and
from the said oak runing South: and
bounding on the said Swamp: one hundred ninety and eight perches: to a
marked oak by the head of a dry Vally
aboue the head of the said swamp and
from thence continuing the Same Course
South by a line of marked trees: one hundred twenty and two perches to a corner
marked white oak standing nigh Unto y^e
head of another dry Valley and from y^t.
oak West by a line of marked trees two
hundred perches to another corner
marked white oak: Standing by the
South side of the head of another dry

Vally: and from thence North by a line of marked trees: Sixty and four perches to a small run. and from thence North^rly downe the severall courses of the said Run: to a corner marked white oak: Standing on the East Side of the mouth of the said Run: By the Creek side: and from thence Easterly downe the said Creek to the first mentioned corner oak:

(13)

Ellis Humphery Land

Surveyed: the 29th day of November 1675: for George Axton two hundred acres of land scituate on the West side of Delaware River: and on ye South side of S^t. Georges Creek: Betweene the two maine branches of a Swamp Called the Doctors Swamp Being bounded as followeth: Viz^t: Begining at a corner marked white oak: Standing in the fork at the dividing of ye said Swamp and from the said oak runing Up the Westerne branc[h] of the said swamp which divideth this from the land of William Marriott South West: forty perches: West South West one hundred Seaventy six perches: and South South West: Eighty six perches: to a corner marked Hickory standing nigh Unto the Eastward side of y[e] head of the said branch and from the said Hickory Runing East South East by a line of marked trees: one hundred and thirty perches to y[e] head of another branch Being the Southermost branch of the afforesaid swamp which divideth this from the land of Doct[r] Spry: and from thence downe the severall courses of the said swamp to the first mentioned white oak:

This belongs to Hermanus Alricks

Surveyed: y[e] 29th: day of Novemb[r]: 1675: for Will[m] Marrio[t] one hundred acres of land scituate on y[e] west side of

Delawa[re] River: and on ye South side
of St Georges Creek: Betweene two
branches of a Swamp called ye Doct^{rs}
swamp being bounded as followeth: Viz^t:
begining at a corn^r m^rked white oak:
standing at ye head of a branch of ye s^d.
swamp (being ye uppermost corn^r tree of
ye land of Bernard Egbert: and from y^e
said oak runing North East by a line of
m^rked trees dividing this from ye land
of the said Bernard: 160 perches to
another corn^r m^rked white oak standing
at the South side of another branch of
the said Swamp and from y^t oak runing
downe ye branch South Easterly: 50
degrees: 90 perches: and North Easterly
83 degrees: 65 perches to ye point of the
fork at ye dividing of ye aforesaid two
branches and from ye said point Up y^e
Westerne branch which divideth this
from ye land of George Axton: to the
place of begining.

(14)

Surveyed: the 7th: day of December 1675 for Peter Thomason two hundred and twenty Acres of Land Scituate on the West side of Delaware river Upon a branch of Christina Creek called white Clayes Creek; aboue the fall thereof: on the Upper side of the land of John Nomers: Being bounded as followeth: (Viz^t. begining at a corn^r m^rked Gum tree Standing at the South side of the maine Run and from the said Gum runing South by a line of m^rked trees: dividing this from ye land of John Nomers: 20 perches to a corn^r m^rked white oak and from the said oak S W by W: by a line of marked trees: 200 perches, to a corner marked white oak standing betweene five small Creeples and from that oak N W by N: by a line of marked trees) 180 perches to a corner marked white oak Standing on a peice of high ground on the North Side

of this said run and from that oak: N E by
E By a line of marked trees: 220 perches
to a corner marked Hickory and from the
Said Hickory S: E: by S: By a line of
marked trees 136 perches: to a corner
marked white oak Standing on a high
bank at the North side of the aforesaid
great run being ye upper corner oak of the
land of the aforesaid Nomers and from
thence South Westerly 4 degrees: (Slanting over ye run and bounding on ye land
of ye said Nomers) 32 perches to the first
mentioned Gum tree: Conteyneing the
said quantity of Land:

(15)

Surveyed: the 26th: day of November
1675: for Richard Staggs 300 acres of
land Scituate on the Westward side of
Delaware river and on the Southeast side
of the Southwes[t] Branch of St Georges
Creek being bounded as followeth Viz^t

begining at a corn^r m^rked white oak: standing at ye s^d bran[ch] side on ye North east side of ye mouth of a small run and from the said oak: runing South east by a line of m^rked trees: dividing this from the land of Bernard Egberts three hundred and 2 perches to a corn^r m^rked white oak Standing by the head of a Branch of a swamp called the Doct^{rs} swamp: and from the said oak South west by a line of marked trees one hundred and fifty perches to a corner marked Hickory and from ye said Hickory N W. by a line of marked trees: three hundred and thirty perches to a corner marked white oak Standing at the head of a small branch from thence downe the branch North 50 perches: North Easterly 8 degrees 34 perches to another corner marked white oak standing on a point at the side of the maine branch: and finally downe ye said maine branch to the first mentioned white oak.

Surveyed: the 4th: day of December 1675: for W[al] ven Johnson: de fox: and Charles Rumsey: five hund[r]ed and seaventy acres of land Scituate on the West side of Delaware river nigh unto the upper end of Bread and Che[ese] Island and on the North West side of white clayes Creek whi[ch] divideth this from the land of John Edmondson being bou[n]ded as followeth Viz^t: begining at a Corn^r marked popler Standing by the Creek's Side a piece of low land nigh unto the upper end of the said Island and from the said popler runing North west by a line of marked trees: 320 perches: to a corner marked black oak: Standing on a piece of falling ground: nigh unto a branch of the said Creek: and from the oak Southwest by a line of marked trees three hundred perch[es] to a corn^r m^{r}ked white oak Standing on ye South west side of [a] Small Swamp and from y^t oak

South east by a line of marked trees two hundred thirty and two perches to a corn^r m^rked Popler [s]tanding at the side of the aforesaid Creek nigh unto ye lower end of a [sm]all Island in ye Creek at ye upper end of the land of John Edmondson (and Faded 3/8 inch) [on] (Torn 1/4 inch) the said Popler runing downe the severall courses of the Said Creek (Torn 1/4 inch) first mentioned Corner marked Popler:

(16)

Surveyed the 6^t day of Decemb^r: 1675: for John Nomers three hundred and forty Acres of land Scituate on the Westward side of Delaware river on both sides of a branch of Christina Creek called white Clayes fall, Being bounded as followeth Viz^t: Begining at a Corner marked Popler at ye side of the maine run: Being a Corner tree of the land of Walraven: Johnson De fox and Charles Rumsey and from the

said Popler runing N: W: By their line
of marked trees: two hundred, thirty, and
two perches: to their upper corner marked
tree Being a white Oak: and from the said
oak S. W: by a line of marked trees: One
hundred fifty and eight perches to a Corner marked white oak: Standing on a high
Banck at the North side of the said run:
and from the Said Oak: South Westerly
four degrees Slanting over the Run: thirty
and two perches: To a corner marked
Gum Tree: Standing at the South side of
the said run: and from the said Gum:
South: twenty perches to a corner marked
white oak: and from that oak South East
by a line of marked trees: two hundred
and   Perches: to a corner marked
white oak: Standing on a barren Levell
and from that oak: N: East: By a line of
marked trees One hundred and twelve
perches to another Corner marked white
oak: and from thence North forty perches

to a Corner marked Maple tree Standing under a high banck by a small Island in the Creek or run: nigh unto the upper Corner tree of the land of John Edmondson and from the said Maple runing downe the Said Run: to ye first mentioned Corner Popler (Excluding the said Island

Surveyed: the 30th: day of July: 1675: John Johnson: James Justason and Peter Hendrickson: five hundred and fifty Acres of land Scituate on the Westward side of Delaware River: Adioyneing to the said River Side Between two Creeks: the one Called Marityes Creek: dividing this from ye Land of Maritye's hook: And the other Called Harwicks Creek: which at the mouth thereof divideth this from the land Called Lemokey Viz^t: begining at Marityes Creek at the Southermost Corner of John Johnsons Cow-

(17)

-house; By the
Side of the path which goeth through y^e
sw[amp] (Torn ¼ inch) to the lowermost
landing of the said Creek: And from
thence Runing by the Swamp or Creeple
which lieth along by the River side N E
by N. 42 perches: North Easterly: 69:
degrees. North 13: perches: North Easterly 79: degrees (over a Swamp) 22:
perches: N: E: by E: 20 perches N E: 66:
degrees: 90: perches N E: (over a Swamp:)
16: perches: E N E: 46 perches: East 35:
perches: E N E: 60 perches: to Harwicks
Creek: then North 20 Perches and N W
by N: 52 Perches up by the Creek and
from the Creek N: W: by a line of marked
trees 25 perches to a Corner marked
black oak Standing nigh unto y[e] head
of a small Swamp: and from the Said
oak: Runing W: S: W: By a line of

marked trees: 248: Perches to a Corn[r]
marked Maple tree Standing in a branch
of Marityes Creek and from thence along
ye said branch South Easterly 6 degrees
50: perches: to the Creek and finally
downe the severall course[s] of the Said
Creek: to the maine river side Conteyneing the said quantity of land besides the swamp and Sunken ground
thereto Adioyneing: three hundred acres
part hereof being forme[rly] granted: unto
the said John Johnson, James Justason
[and] (Faded ½ inch) John Hendrickson:
Each one hundred Acres By three
[patents][8] (Faded ½ inch) But not one
concurring with the Scituation of the
p[lace] (Torn ½ inch) all beareing date
the 20th: day of April 1673: Since [which]i
(Torn ¾ inch) time Peter Hendrickson
is invested in the Right [of] the Said

---

[8] Supplied from text in George Smith, *Hist. Del. Co.*
(1862) 522.

John Hendrickson) and two hundred and
fifty [acres] (Torn ¾ inch) the other part
hereof Being New land:[9]

Surveyed (the 27th: day of July: 1675)
for Charles Jans[on]: Olie Rawson: Olie
Nielson: Hans Hopman: John Hendrickson and Hans Olieson: A tract of land
Called Marities hook: Scituate and being
on the Westward side of Delaware river
Being bounded as followeth (Viz[t]) Begining at a small point of the high land within the mouth of Naamans Creek: And
from thence Runing North by west one
hundred twenty and three perches: and
North two hundred perches: Bounded
with the Creek to a Corner marked white
oak: By the Creek side at the mouth of a
small branch: And from thence E by N
bounded with the said Branch: And with
a line of marked trees: from the head of

---

[9] This survey printed with slight variants in George Smith,
Hist. Del. Co. Pa. (Phila., 1862), pp. 521–522.

the Branch to a Corner marked Spanish Oak Stan[ding] By a small Run: three hundred and eighty perches

(18)

thence North North East along the Run: thirty two perches: to a corner marked white oak Standing at ye side of Marities Creek at the lower side of the mouth of the said run: and from thence downe the severall Courses of the Creek to the maine River side, and from thence downe along the river Side to the place of Begining at the mouth of Naamans Creek: Conteyneing and laid out for one thousand Acres of land which was formerly granted unto the Said persons in the time of the Dutch Government:

Surveyed (the 21^t day of february 1675: for Michaell ffredericks two parcells of land: Conteyneing in the whole: three hundred Acres: Scituate on the West-

ward side of Delaware river: Between the
land Called Pimeepahka: and the land
of Towocawomink: (Viz^t) two hundred
Acres part hereof: Begining at a corner
marked Black oak: by the river side:
which divideth this from the land of Peter
Peterson and Gasper ffish: and from the
said Oak Runing N N W: By their line
of Marked three hundred and twenty
perches: to their Upper Corner bounded
tree being a black Oak: and from the
Said oak W S W: By a line of marked
trees: One hundred perches to another
Corner marked Black oak and from
thence S S E: by a line of marked trees:
three and twenty perches to a corn^r
marked white oak: Standing by the
River side: and from thence E: N E:
along the River side to the first mentioned
corner oak: And one hundred Acres the
Residue hereof begining at a corner
marked beech Standing on a Small point

at the mouth of Sissowokissink Creek and from thence Runing E N E forty perches and N E by E one hundred and fourteene perches (By the River side) to a Corner Marked Black oak at the side of a small Creek; And from the Said Oak; N N W: By a line of marked trees: two hundred and Sixty perches to a Corner marked white oak: Standing by the maine Run: of Sissowokissink Creek: And from the Said white Oak: downe along the said Run and Creek Dividing this from the land of Towocawomink: to the first Mentioned Beech tree

(19)

Surveyed: the 30th: day of Octob[r]: 1675 for ffrancis W[att] (Torn ¼ inch) and Dunk Williams: four hundred and fifty Acres of Land Called Point pleasant: Scituate on the Westward Side of Delaware River; and on the lower Side of the

Nishambane Creek: about a Mile and halfe Up the said Creek: Begining at a Corner marked Black Oak: Standing on a point at t[he] (Faded ⅟₁₆ inch) Mouth of a Small branch or Runn: and from thence ru[n]ing North West, along the Run forty Perches to a Corner marked white oak: standing by the Runs Side; and from that oak: North by a line of marked trees: three hundred and Sixty perches: to a Corner Marked white Oak Standing on a Levell: And from that East North East By a line of Marked trees: two hundred and forty perches to a Corn^r marked Birch tree: Standing at the Side of the Maine Creek And from thence downe the Severall Courses of the said Creek to the first mentioned Corn^r Oak: Conteyneinge the said Quantity of Land:

Surveyed (the tenth day of September 1675) for Hendrick Coleman And Peter

Putcan, One hundred [acres] (Torn ½ inch) of Land: Scituate on the Westward Side of Delaware River and on the North West side of a Creek: Called the Mill Creek: over against: Karraconks hook, being bounded [as] (Torn ⅛ inch) followeth (Viz^t: Begining at a Corn^r marked white oak Standing nigh unto the Creek Side; Being a bounded tree Betwixt this land and y^e land of Calcoon hook: and from thence Runing N N W: By a line of Marked Trees dividing this from the said Calcoon-hook Land Two hundred and Ninety perches; to a Corn= marked Red Oak: And from [y^t] (Torn ¼ inch) Oak: E N E: By a Line of Marked Trees: One hundr[ed] twenty and eight perches to a Corn^r marked Black oak: Sta[nding] (Faded ½ inch) on the Side of a hill: By a Branch of the said Creek Call[ed] Mohorhoottinks: And from thence downe

y^e Said branch [and] (Faded ¼ inch)
Creek to the first mentioned Corn^r oak:[10]

(20)

March ye first: 1675:

Surveyed for Jurian Hartsfelder a
Parcell of Land Called Hartsfield scituate and being on ye Westward side: of
Delaware River at the lower Side of
Cohocksinks Creek: begining at ye mouth
of a small Creek: or Run Called Called
Cooah-que-nau-que: and from thence
Runing Up ye severall Courses of the
said Runn to the North end of Cooah-
que-nauque bridge: and from thence
North by West: along by the West side
of a piece of Meadow ground, one hundred and twelve perches to a Corn^r
marked black oak standing at the uper
end of the said Meaddow Ground: from

---

[10] Printed with slight variants in George Smith, *Hist. Del. Co. Pa.* (Phila., 1862) p. 522.

thence North East; one hundred Eighty and four perches (By a line of Marked trees; to a Corn[r] Marked white oak: Standing at y[e] South West side of a branch: of Cohocksinks Creek: from thence downe along the severall Courses of the said branch and Creek: to the maine River Side: and finally downe by the River Side to the place of begining Conteyneing and laid out for three hundred and fifty acres of Land.

[11]Surveyed the 20th day of September 1675: for Cap[t] Hans Monson: the tract of land where he now dwells; Called Oronemink: scituate on y[e] Westward Side of Delaware River: and on the West side of the Schuyle Kill: Being bounded as followeth (Viz[t]) Beginging at a corn[r] marked white oak Standing att y[e] Side of the

11–11 Printed in George Smith, *Hist. Del. Co. Pa.* (Phila., 1862) p. 523. Listed in *Duke of York Record*, p. 55.

Said Kill: Aboue ye mouth of a Creek:
Called the great Queen fall: And from
the said oak runing North West By a line
of Marked trees: One hundred Seaventy
and three perches to a corner marked
white Oak: Standing at the side of a
small Branch: of ye said Creek: and from
that oak: West By a line of marked trees:
Two hundred twenty and two perches:
to a Corner Marked white oak: Standing
at the head of a Branch of Karraconks
Mill Creek: Which Branch is by y^e
Indians called Amiseecauminks and from
ye said oak runing downe along ye said
branch and maine run: to another corn^r
marked black oak: standing at ye South
side of the s^d run or Creek, ye distance
(South Westerly 4 degrees: by a line of
marked trees: one hundred & ten perches
to a corn^r marked black oak: standing by
a small swamp: and from thence E.S.
(Torn ½ inch) E^t: By a line of marked

trees: 300^h forty and six perches to a corn^r, marked white oak: Standing on a small point nigh unto ye head of Inkhorns Creek: and from thence along Inkhornes Creek to ye Schuyle Kill and from ye mouth of Inkhornes Creek: along [b]y ye side of the Schuyle Kill to ye first mentioned corner oak: Conteyneing Eleven hundred Acres of Land:———Which was formerly granted unto y^{esd} Capt Mounson: for one hundred acres (more or less) By patent bearing date ye 10th of March (Faded ½ inch)[11]

(21)

Aprill ye 22th: 1676
Tho: Sawyers Land
[12]Surveyed: for Abraham Enloes A parcell of land Called Abrahams delight,

---

[12-12] Printed with slight variants in *Duke of York Record*, pp. 33–34.

Scituate and being on the West side of
Delaware River and on the North side of
St Augustines Creek: Next adioyneing to
ye land of Mr Peter Aldricks: Begining at
a corner marked white oak standing on a
point in ye first fork of the said Creek:
And from the said Oak: Runing N: E^t: 68
pearches North sixty four perches and
North Wester^ly: 58: degre[es] two hundred twenty and three perches: Bounding
on the Northern Branch to a Corner
marked white oak Standing on a Small
point Between the two head Branches of
the Said Northern branch: from thence
S by W: By a line of marked trees, Sixty
and two perches, to a Corn^r marked white
oak: Stan[d]ing at the East side of the
head of a swamp which proceedeth out
of ye maine branch of St Augustines
Creek. And from thence downe the severall Courses of the said Swamp and
Creek to ye first mentioned^wt oak Con-

teyneing and now laid out for one hundred and Seaventy Acres of Land[12]:

"by me   Walter Wharton
By order and appointment of
Capt. Edmond Cantwell
Surveyor General"[13]

Isaac * * *

[14]Surveyed: May ye 16th: 1676: for Morrice Daniell a parcell of land called Dumers neck Scituate and being on the West side of Delaware river, and on the Northwest side of Appoquenemink Creek: Begining at a Corn^r marked white oak Standing on a point by the said Creek: at ye Upper side of a branch: which at the mouth thereof divideth this from the land of Bernard Hendrickson and from the said oak runing Up the Branch North North West forty perches and then North West By the Said Bernards line of marked

---

[13] Additional from *Duke of York Record*, p. 34.

[14–14] Printed with variants in *Duke of York Record*, pp. 34-35.

trees: four hundred and eighty perches to a Corn[r] marked Hickory: from thence South West By a line of marked trees: Sixty perches to a corn[r] mark[d] Red oak: being y[e] Upper corner tree of a parcell of land formerly to Jacob Hiadn: from thence South East By the said Jacobs line of Marked trees four hundred perches into a Swamp: And then downe Swamp South South East: Sixty perches to y[e] aforesaid Creek: and finally downe [a]long y[e] Creek to y[e] first mentioned white Oak conteyneing One hundred [a]nd ninety acres of land w[ch] was formerly granted Unto John B[r]adborn By patent bearing date y[e] 17th day of June 1671 and By him deserted.[14]

"by me Walter Wharton
By Order and appointment of
Capt. Edmond Cantwell
Surveyor Generall
17th June 1671.
Survey of Land for Morris Daniel"][15]

---

[15] Additional from *Duke of York Record*, p. 35.

(22)

Aprill the 24th: 1676: Hybert Lawrens Land

Surveyed: for Mr Casparus Herman a Tract or parcell of land Called the good neighbour: Scituate and Being on the West side of Delaware River and on ye North East side of S^t. Augustines Creeke; begining att a corner marked white Oak: Standing on a point: Att the uper side of ye mouth of a Branch or Swamp and from the head thereof, By a line of marked trees: One hundred and fifty perches: to the line of George Axton nigh Unto a Corner marked Hickory standing a litle out of the line: By the head of a small Swamp and from thence West North West By a line of marked trees three hundred and Seaventy perches: to a Corner marked White oak; Standing on a levell; and from thence South West

by South By a line of marked trees:
three hundred perches to a Corner Marked
Maple Standing at the North side of the
maine Branch of St Augustines Creek:
And from thence downe along the said
Branch and Creek: to the first mentioned
White Oak Conteyneing three hundred
and thirty acres of Land:

May ye 24th: 1676:

Surveyed then for John Barker a parcell of Land Called Culton Scituate and
being on ye West side of Delaware River
and on the North Side of a branch of
Blackbird Creek which divideth this the
Land of Capt Matthias Nicholls and
Mr Tho: Louelace Begining at a corner
marked Hickory: Standing at the side
of the said Branch By a Beaver Dame
it being the Upper Corner tree of the
land of John Hartoy: And from thence
runing North By the said Hartoys line

of marked trees; Two hundred forty and Six perches: to a Corner mark^d White oak: And from thence West by a line of marked trees One hundred and fifty perches: to a Corner marked Gum: Standing the side of a Poquoson: from thence South By a Line of marked trees two hundred and thirty perches to a Corner Marked Maple: Standing at the Side of the Said branch; And from thence downe along the run of the

(23)

Said Branch to the first mentioned Corner tree: Con-[teyne]ing two hundred and twenty Acres of Land:

Aug^st: ye 10th 1676:

Laid out for Mr Johannes Dehaes a Lott of ground Scituate and being in New Castle upon Delaware River Being

Bounded on the South West wth ye Lott of Samuell Land; on the North East with a Lott then laid out for Walter Wharton, on the South East with Land street and on the North West: with Minquaa's Street: Conteyneing in Breadth at both ends: Sixty foot and a halfe and in lenght (on both sides from Street to Street,) three hundred foot:

August: ye 10th: 1676:

Laid out for William Orion a Lott of ground Scituate and Being in New Castle upon Delaware River, Being bounded on the South West with the land of Walter Wharton; On ye North East: with ye lott of John Ogle; On the South East with the land Street on ye North West: with Minquaa's Street: Conteyneing in Breadth at both ends; Ninety foot and and in length on both Sides from Street to Street three hundred foot

August the 10th: 1676:

Laid out for John Ogle a lott of ground
Scituate and being in New Castle upon
Delaware River: Being Bounded on the
South West: with the lott of William
Orion on

(24)

North East with a Lott of waste
ground: on ye South East: with Land
Street and on the North West with Minquaa's street Conteyneing in Breadth
at both Ends: Sixty foot and in lenght
on both sides from Street to Street three
hundred foot

August ye 10th: 1676:

Laid out for Mr John Williamson Nerring a Lot of ground Scituate and being
in New Castle Upon Delaware River
Being bounded on the South West with
the Lott of Mrs Sarah Out Hout: and on

the North East with the Lott of Gysbert Derickson; On the South East with Land Street, and on the North West with Minuaas Street: Conteyneing in breadth at both ends: sixty foot, and in Lenght (on both sides from Street to Street, three hundred foot:

August ye 10th: 1676:

Laid out for Ghysbert Derickson a Lott of ground Scituate in New Castle Upon Delaware River: being bounded on ye South West: with the land of John Williamson Nerring on the North East with the old fort Street: On the South east with land Street: And on the North West: With Minquaas Street: Conteyneing in breadth (at both ends) Sixty foot and in lenght (on both sides from Street to Street three hundred foot

August y^e. 9th: 1676:

Laid out for Mr Samuell Land a lott of

ground Scituate & Being in New Castle
Upon Delaware River being bounded

(25)

On the South West with the Land of
Mr John Moll: on the North east with
the lott of Mr Johannes Dehaes, on the
So[uth] East With land Street; and on
the North West with Minquaa'[s] Street
Conteyneing in Breadth at Both ends:
Sixty foot and a halfe; and in length on
both sides from Street to Street three
hundred foot;

August ye 10th: 1676:

Laid out for Walter Wharton a Lott
of Ground Scituate & being in New Castle
Upon Delaware River Being bounded on
the South West with ye Lott of M^r
Johannes Dehaes: on the North east with
the Lott of William Orion; on the South
East With land Street and on the North

West with Minquaa's Street: Conteyneing in breadth at both ends Sixty foot and
a halfe; and in lenght on both Sides: three
hundred foot

August: ye 10th: 1676;

Laid out for Mrs Sarah Out-Hout a
Lott of ground Scituate And being in
New Castle Upon Delaware River: being
Bounded on the South West with a lott
of Wast ground lying Between this and
the lott of John Ogle; on ye North East
with the Lott of John Williamson Nerring
One the South East with Land Street and
on the North Est with Minquaa's Street:
Conteyneing in breadth at both ends sixty
foot, & in length on both sides from
Street to Street, three hundred foot.

(26)

July ye 7th: 1676:

Surveyed for John Clark a parcell of
land Called Darby scituate and Being on

the West side of Delaware River and on
the Northward Side of St Georges Creek:
Adioyneing to the West side of the land
of Mr Jacob Young: Begining at a corner
marked Spanish oak: Standing at ye side
of the maine branch of the said Creek,
being the Upper corn^r tree of the Said
Mr Young's Land: And from thence runing North along Mr Young's line (three
hundred twenty and Eight perches: to
his Corner marked white oak: standing
at ye Side of the Dragon Swamp: from
thence (following the said Swamp: West
thirty two perches: South by West
eighteene perches: West by South: one
hundred Seaventy and two perches: And
South Westerly: forty degrees: thirty &
eight perches to a Corner marked Gum
tree: Standing By the head of a Small
branch: from thence South: 30: Perches
to a Corner marked Red oak: Standing
by Mr Youngs Cart-way: from thence

South East: By a line of marked trees:
ninety six perches to a corner marked
Gum tree Standing at the head of a
Branch of the Said Creek: Called Rattle
Snake branch: And from the Said Gum
following the said branch and Creek to
the first mentioned: Spanish Oak: Conteyneing and laid out for three hundred
acres of Land:

Aprill ye 21st: 1676:

Surveyed for Mr Pieter Aldricks: a
tract of land Called Grooningen: Scituate
and Being on the West side of Delaware
River; and on the North East side of S^t
Augustines Creek: Begining at a corner
marked black oak Standing on the near-
est point (of Wood land) Unto the Said
Creek by the River Side And from thence
runing North east: Ninty four perches:
North Easterly thirty degrees Seaventy
eight perches: North North East: fifty
two perches

(27)

North Easterly fifteene degrees Seaventy two perches: No[rth] North East eighty & six perches North East and by North one hundred eighty and six perches (Bounding Upon the maine River Unto the Mouth of a small Creek (or Sprout) Called litle St Georges Creek, Which divideth this from the Land of Mrs Ann Wale: And from thence West: 40 perches S W by W one hundred fifty and three perches and North Westerly 73 degrees one hundred forty and six perches: Bounding Upon ye Said Creek or Sprout, to M^{rs}. Wales line of Marked trees: C (Faded ¼ inch) ing the Said Branch; And from thence W. S. W. along the said Mrs Wales line of marked trees: one hundred forty and two perches, to her Upper corner trees: Being a White oak Standing nigh Unto the head of a Swamp: which proceedeth out of the

Northern Branch of S[t] Augustunes Creek:
and fro[m] thence downe along the
severall Courses of the said branch and
Marsh to the first mentioned Black oak,
Conteyne[ing] and now laid out for five
hundred and Sixty acres of Land:

June y[e] 27th: 1676:

Surveyed for M[r] John Moll a Tract of
land Called Moles hole: scituate and
Being on y[e] West side of Delaware River:
Between y[e] Said River and a great swamp
Called Dragon Swamp And next Adioyneing Unto the land of M[r] Henry Ward:
Begining at a Corner Marked Spanish
oak: Standing at y[e] North east side of a
branch of y[e] Said Dragon Swamp: (it
being y[e] Upper Corner tree of the land of
the Said Ward: And from thence runinge
North Easterly: 47 degrees: along the
Said Wards line: (one hundred Sixty and
two perches: to a Corner Marked white

oak Standing by the side of a swamp or Creeple: (which lyeth betweene this land, And the River and is also another corner tr[ee] of the land of the said Wards: And from thence following ye Severall Courses of the said swamp: (or Creeple: to a corner Marked white oak; standing at the head of a Beaver Dame bran[ch] and from thence Runing West By a line of Marked trees four hundred and forty perches: to a corner Marked White Oak Standing on the East side of the head of a branch of the Said Dragons Swamp: And from thence following the seve[rall]

(28)

Courses of the said Branch and Dragon Swamp to the first mentioned Spanish oak: Conteyneing and laid out for one thousand acres of Land: Six hundred acres part hereof Being formerly granted Unto William Currer and William Gold-

smith: By Pattent Beareing date the
fifteenth day of January: 1675: Since
Which time Mr John Moll is invested in
their Right: And the other four hundred
acres beinge New Land:

April: the 1th: 1676

Surveyed for John Ogle and John
Garretson a certaine parcell of land
Scituate and Being on the West Side of
Delaware river and on the South side of
Christina Creek next to the Upper side
of Swartnutt Island being Bounded as
followeth Begining on a small point of
firme Land at the Mouth of a Branch or
Small Creek: which divideth land from
the said Island and from thence runing
North Easterly eighty Seaven degrees
(over a Swamp along the said small Creek
fifty two perches and East twelve perches
to a Corner Marked Black oak: Standing

on a point at the mouth of a small swamp from thence Runing Up the said Swamp: South by West eighty perches: S: E: 15: Perches: South Easterly 27 degrees thirty and two perches: and East and by South: 20 perches to a Corner Marked Maple Standing at the head of the said Swamp: from thence S. E. by a line of Marked trees two hundred perches to a Corner Marked Red oak: from thence S: W: By a line of Marked trees: two hundred perches to a Corner Marked Hickory: from thence N: W: By a line of Marked trees: three hundred Fifty and eight perches to a corner Marked Gum tree Standing at the Side of Christina Creek: And from thence downe along the severall Courses of Christina Creek to the place of begining: Conteyneing four hundred and forty acres of Land: As by a Map of ye Same hereto Anexed may more plainly

Appeare: One hundred Acres part hereof, Being formerly granted Unto James Crawford: By patent Bearing date ye first day of January: 1667; and three hundred And forty Acres; the residue being new Land.

(29)[16]

> By vertue of a warrant from y^e
> Co^rt of new Castle bearing Date
> y^e   Day of

Laid out a Lott of grounde for Moyses Degon (Faded 1 inch) in ye Towne of new on a Street Called Land Street being bond on ye southwest wth ye house & Lott of Joannes Dehaes to ye northeast wth ye Lott of John boyer to ye south East wth Land Street to ye northwest wth minquas street Longe boath sides 300 foott & broad

---

[16] Pages 29–33 are in the hand of contemporary Surveyor Captain Edmund Cantwell, of New Castle. The index is in another contemporary hand.

before & behend 69 foott Laid on ye 10 Day of July 1679.

⸿ Ed Cantwell:—

By vertue of a warrant from ye Co^rt of new Castle bearing Date y^e   Day of   167 Laid out a Lott of grounde for John boyer Situate in ye Towne of new Castle in a Streett Called Land Streett being bond to ye southwest wth ye Lott of Moyses (Torn ¼ inch) g and to ye north East wth ye Lott of henrik van der burgh to ye South East wth Land Streett to ye northwest wth menquas streett Longe boath sides 300 foott & broad before & behend 62 foott Laid out ye 20 Day of July 1679:—

⸿ Ed Cantwell:—

By vertue of a warrant from ye Co^rt of new Castle bearing Date ye 8 Day of 9^br 1678:—

Laid out for Englabert Lott two Lott of gronde situated in ye Towne of new Castle & att ye north East end thereof one of wch Lotts being that whereon ye ould foart stood ye other being a Lott formely Laid for henrik van der bugh being bonded as followeth to ye South west wth ye high way or Streett wch Lead to y^e

(Faded ¾ inch)

(30)

to ye north East wth ye Comon not as yet taken up to ye South East wth ye Streett by ye water Side to ye northwest wth Land Streett being Longe to ye Southwest next ye high way two hondered & Seveanny & Sevean foott to ye north East two hondered & Sixty Eight foott being broad before & behend two hondered & twenty foott wth Exspresse Condiction that ye said Lott shall Levill & make even ye ould foart & Leave a Sufficient Street or high way att ye water side Laid out ye 24 Day of may 1679

         ⚶ Ed Cantwell:—

7br ye 2th Day 1675:

Laid out for henrick Taden one peace or p^r sell of Land Situated Lying & being on the west side [of] Delawar River & on a Creeke Commonly knowne (Torn 1 inch) land on Mill Creek it being the Land whereon he Dwelleth the said Land begening at a Corner Marke Spanish oak standing by a Creeke Comonly Knowne & Called   Creek [wi]ch Runing in to the woods north west & by west 320 pearches it being the Devission Line wch partes this Land from belonging to (Faded 1 inch) to a white oak then south west and by wes 140 pearches to a Corn^r marked black oak then sout east & by east 320 pearches to a Marked spanish oak w^s divides this from the Land of ✠ * * * (Erased and faded 3 inches) of Land More or Lesse

(31)

✠then north east & by East 140 pearches
to the first place of begining being Laid
out for 280 acres of Land More or Lesse

℔ Ed Cantwell:

7br yᵉ 2 Day 1675

[17]Laid out for henrick John & Bartell
Esskells two peace or persells of Land
Situated Lying & being on the west side
of Delawar River on a Creek Runing out
of the said River Comonly Knowe &
Called Ams Land or Mill Creek the one
peace of Land begining at a Conʳ of a
frisch wᶜʰ devides & partes henrick
Thatens Land from this Land Runing
north west & by west in to the woods
320 pearches to a Cornʳ mʳked white oake
then north east & by east 131½ pearch
to a Corner mrked black oake then South
South East 320 pearches to a Smake stony
Runn wᶜʰ partes John Cornelis & Marton
Martosen for this Land then Southwest

& by west to first place of bengining 130½ pearches the other peace of p^rsell of Land Lying & being on the South Side of henrick Thadens Land begining at a Corn^r marked spanish oake by a Run called Stony Run then Runing out in to the woods 320 pearches to a corner marked Black oak, dividing[18] (illegible 2 inches) it from Tadens Land then southwest & by west 308 pearches to the Creeke Called Crume Kill then allong the Crom Kill the severall Courses of the Creek Kill & sampe to a smal stake runing out of Crom Kill 500 pearches then north east & by east to the first place of being 136 pearches boath peaces or p^rsell of Land being Laid out for 154: acres more or Lesse.[17]

⚭ Ed Cantwell

[17–17] Printed with some variants and errors in George Smith, *Hist. Del. Co., Pa.* (Phila., 1862) p. 522.

[18] Supplied from Smith, p. 522.

(32)

7br yᵉ 2ᵗʰ Day 1675:

[20]Laid out for henrick Thadens one peace or pʳsell of Land whereon he now Dwelleth Situated Lying & being one the west side of Delawar River in a Creeke Comonly Knowne & Called Ams Land or Mill Creek & betwen two peaces of Land belonging to henrich Johnson & bartell Esscells begining[19] (illegible 1 inch) at a Cornʳ of a fench wᶜʰ divids this Land from the Land of amsland Runing in to the woods north west & by west 320: pearches to a cornʳ marked white oake then southwest & by west 140 pearches to a Corner mʳked black oak then South East & by South 320 pearches to a Cornʳ marked Spanish oak Standing by the Mouth of a Run Called Stony Rune then

---

[19] Word supplied from Smith, p. 523.

[20]-[20] Printed with slight variants in George Smith, *Hist. Del. Co. Pa.* (Phila., 1862) p. 523.

then north East & by East 140 pearches
to the first place of begining Conteyned
& Laid out for 280 acres or more or Lesse:

℔ Ed Cantwell:[20]

[ ]br ye 2th. Day 1675:

[21]Laid out for John Cornelis & Marteon
Marteson Snio^r one peace or pesell of
Land wherein they now Dwelleth Situ-
ateth Lying & Being on ye west side of
Delawar River & one a Creek wch Coms
out of the said River Comonly knowne
and Called amsland or Mill Kill begining
at a small stonye Rune wch Devides this
Land from henrisch Johnson & Bartell
Esskells Runing in to the woods north-
werd & by west 320 pearches to a Corn^r
m^rked black oake then north East by
East 400 pearches to a Corn^r Marked
black oak Standing by a Creek Called
mockoronipatte then alonge the severall
Courses of the Creeke

[21–21] Printed with slight variants in Smith, p. 522.

(33)

to the Mouth thereof 320 pearches then allonge the Mill Creek to the first place of begining 300 pearches Conteyned Laid out for 728 acres More or Lesse

℈ Ed Cantwell:[21]

INDEX

By
FRANK L. BATTAN
Longwood, Kennett Square, Pa.

INDEX